THE BIRTH AND EVOLUTION OF THE SOUL

THE BIRTH AND EVOLUTION OF THE SOUL

BY
ANNIE BESANT

GYAN

ISBN: 978-81-212-1914-3 (HB)
First Published, 1895
Published, 2018
Published by

Gyan Publishing House
5, Ansari Road
Daryaganj, New Delhi-110002
Phone: 011-47034999, 9811692060
www.gyanbooks.com
E-mail: books@gyanbooks.com

Printed at: G. Print Process, Delhi.

The Birth & Evolution of the Soul.

PART I.

THESE two lectures might better perhaps be described as one lecture in two parts, for I am really going to try and give you in the two a connected tracing of the progress of the soul. There is so much confusion in thought as to the origin of the individual, as to what the individual really means, as to how he is developed, and what is to be his ultimate destiny, that I thought I could take no better subject for a Lodge, which ought to be a Lodge of students, than to trace out somewhat in detail this most important matter in the light of Theosophy. Important, because on it turns your whole view of the purpose of the Universe; and if the growth of the Soul were better understood than it is, we should not hear the continual questions asked as to why there should be a Universe at all, and why there should be manifestation; why, if everything comes out of One and goes back to One again, why this intermediate condition of multiplicity should occur. The whole of these questions really turn on misunderstanding, or on lack of accurate knowledge, and it is to the clearing up of that misunderstanding that I am going to address myself to-night and this night week.

In order to make the origin of the individual clear, I must ask you to come back with me to the time when the human race was evolving, but when as yet the individual had not come into existence. Come back to what you know, in Theosophical literature, as the first Race of man. You may remember that—according to the teachings which you find in *The Secret Doctrine* and in the great Scriptures of the world—you may remember that the first Race had its bodies built up, as it were, round a form that is said to have been derived from the Moon. The Pitris, or ancestors, who afforded the first matrix for humanity, who give the first ethereal form through and by the help of which the physical in man was to evolve—those are spoken of as the Lunar Pitris because of their connection with the Moon. Into that connection I have not time to go in detail, but the traces of it are around you on every side at the present time. You must be perfectly well aware that the effect of the Moon upon the Earth is marked and constant; and, above all, you may notice that it is the measure in time of all great physiological periods. The fact that you still find that to be the case after so many millions of years should make it at least not surprising to you when you read in ancient books that there is a causal relation between the Moon and the Earth, and between the ancestors of humanity and forms of living beings who existed on the lunar globe in ages gone by.

Now, these Lunar Pitris that came and projected their astral forms, as it is said, in order that the first Race of man might develop, came to the Earth, this Earth on which we are now, which is the central globe in the ring of globes, and they came to it—so far as we need trouble about it to-night—for the Fourth Round; of course not for the first time, but I am ignoring the first three Rounds. When they arrived at this globe for the Fourth Round they threw out these shadows—ethereal bodies, as they are called. The reason—and I may as well mention it in passing—why an ethereal body, or body of astral matter, should in point of time come before the physical body that we know, is that you cannot have any vital energies at work, you cannot have any electrical or magnetic currents, or any of those currents which have to do with the various phenomena of life and of chemical action, without the presence of ether. So that it is not possible to draw together physical molecules for the making of a dense body unless you have what we may call a matrix of ether through which these forces are able to act, and so to draw together, and hold together after they are drawn, the physical molecules. In fact, every physical molecule has its envelope of ether, and is permeated therewith, and it is by means of this ethereal envelope of the molecule that these life-forces are able to draw and hold the physical body together.

During the first and second Races of man this physical body was built up by the action of what are called Nature-Spirits, who made this outer clothing of man, the tabernacle of flesh, as it is sometimes entitled. Out of the first Race evolved the second, and out of the second evolved the third. No break, nothing that would be called a new creation, but definite and sequential evolution. The materials used in these bodies had been worked up in previous ages through mineral and vegetable and animal, and so had taken on, as far as their atoms were concerned, an internal differentiation, which is of enormous importance when they enter into the body of the higher animals and of man.

Man, again, is nearly the first being that appears on this globe at the stage of evolution that we are considering. Pass, then, from the first and second Races to the third. When the third Race was evolving, slowly and gradually through almost incalculable periods of time, the animal development took place; that is, the development of the physical and astral bodies went on during the first and second Races, and in the third that of the body of sensation, as you know it in yourselves and in the lower animals, the body which receives and translates into feeling all impressions from without. Your outside body receives contacts from the external universe, and certain parts of it are modified to answer to those contacts; these modified parts we call the sense-organs. But you are aware that the sense-organ in the body, while it answers by way of vibration to any vibration of its own particular class that comes to it from without, is not that which feels or perceives. This vibration has to be transmitted inwards in a very real sense, and not only inwards to the sense-centres, as they are called, in the brain, but inwards from this again by way of the astral body—and this action shows itself always by the passing of electrical and magnetic currents—into this third body that I am now speaking of, the body of sensation. You may have a break between the outer impact and what we call feeling, between the outer vibrations of the ether on the retina of the eye and what we call sight. The power of sight, the power of tasting, of smelling, of hearing, of feeling, all these powers reside in this body of sensation, and that is, of course, why it has that particular name. Now, the lower animals have this body as well as we. You find it in the animals with which you are familiar around you. They feel, and not only do they feel, but they show emotions, passions and appetites. You will see the passion of anger in some animals; you will see sex passion, you will find hunger, thirst—all these things are present in the lower animals, and we may group them all together, in order that a single phrase may describe these activities as the "body of sensation" or, as it is often called, the "body of desire."

As you are a Lodge of students, I may venture to use a Sanskrit word, the word Kâma. This body is spoken of as the Kâma body, Kâma Rûpa, which is only the Sanskrit for "desire body;" and I use the name because I want in a moment to quote a phrase in which that word Kâma occurs. In the animal it is developed. Now, it is part of the truth of evolution that every stage of an evolving organism contains within itself in germ the next stage by which evolution is to proceed. Take what stage of evolution you like in the outer world, and you will always find that at any stage there is a germ which, if it proceeds, will develop into a new individual. This is characteristic of all forms of living things, and by the improvement from the germ evolution proceeds. You may take vegetable, you may take animal, you may take man, take what you like: always you will find that, if an individual is to be produced, a germ will be present which is to form part-helper of his growth. *Part* helper only; and this is always present in what is called the passive side of Nature.

You remember that if you go right back almost to the beginning of things you find what are called the "pairs of opposites," and the first appearance of these in the Second Logos is often spoken of as being Spirit-Matter, in order to give the two great poles of existence between which all organization takes place. Two characteristics mark those two poles. One of them is active, and the other is passive; one of them is positive, the other is negative; one of them is that which gives impulse, the other is that which gives form; and these two are present everywhere, inseparable in Nature. Right through Nature, not only in physical Nature, but through all realms of Nature, you will find this diversity; and without the union of these two together you will find nowhere fresh growth, progress in evolution. There must always be the stimulating force, and there must be the form that develops. You may call them, if you like, male and female, as in physical Nature; you may call them, if you like, Father and Mother; but keep the idea plainly in mind, because on this the understanding of the origin of the individual soul depends.

Now, let me remind you of the line of evolution, which is the line of form, which comes from the Moon originally, and evolves downwards to Kâma. This, I say, is found in the animal just as it is in man, and you need to keep that in mind. In that Kâma or desire—which builds a body with the power of sensation, the power of not only answering to outside impact, but of translating it into feeling—lies the root of self-consciousness. Consciousness in germ is simply the power to respond to a vibration that comes from outside; and when to that power of response there is added feeling, then you get what we may call the "germ of mind"—not mind, but its germ, the negative side of mind in which and by means of which mind may evolve.

If for a moment you will look at the lower animals you will see a startling difference between the wild and the domesticated. You will find in the domesticated animal very much more of what you would call mind than you find in the wild animal; and for a very simple reason that you will see as we go on.

If you take the wild animal that has never come across man at all, you will find in it plenty of response to the impacts of the external world; but you will find in it comparatively little reasoning, little judgment, little linking together of inner sensation and outer object, unless the object be present, or unless some craving of the organism gives an impulse to action. Food, for instance, being within the sight of an animal, even if it is not very hungry, will cause movement towards the food, or the craving of the organism for sustenance will make it seek for food. But you do not get in the wild animal much of what you may call "ideal action," action without an impulse which comes from bodily necessities, or from the presence of an external object; that is, you have not there present much of what we know as mind, of which the lowest and earliest manifestations are the connection between an outer object and an inner sensation and the power of recalling that connection and acting upon it without the object being present—the qualities which technically are called perception and recollection.

At this stage, then, of this single line that I have brought down thus we have got as far as the development of Kâma, in which is the germ of mind, the stage in which, if there is to be a higher evolution, some impulse from without must be given. The passive side of Nature, brooded over by the Divine Spirit, could not by itself get any further than this stage—the development of a germ; and when you have the body of desire present, that contains in it this germ of mind; think of it now, if you like, as the female or mother side of Nature.

Now, for a moment leaving this altogether, take an analogy from lower Nature. Let me ask any of you who happen to be botanists—and probably all of you know enough of botany to follow the illustration—to take what is called the ovule of a plant, that which develops into a seed; left to itself that ovule which is in the female organ will never be anything more than an ovule: it will simply wither up and perish. But it contains within it all the nourishment by means of which a new plant will grow; it has stored up, as it were, a stock of food, if any new life, an individual, should there begin. But an individual cannot begin there simply by the action of the ovule itself; it needs a stimulus which comes from the contents of the male organ of the plant, the pollen, and if that pollen throws out a minute cell which enters the ovule and comes into contact with the germ cell within the ovule, then there will be an interaction between these two microscopic cells, and by the union of the two a new impulse will be given, and an individual will result which will develop for a time within this ovule which has now become the seed, and after a time will show marks characteristic of its parents; but it will separate itself from the parents and carry on life on its own account, having its own root, its own stem, and its own leaves. The starting-point of that is the junction of the two microscopic cells, differing in their nature—the one positive, impulse-giving, fertilizing; the other receptive, passive, nutrient—showing the characteristics of the two sides of Nature. Now we have here got the passive, nutrient side developed along this line which I characterized as lunar—coming from the moon. It is the side of form, and it may perhaps interest you to notice that it is the side that receives from outside, the passive side again, and that all these emotions and everything else in it are set up in answer to this impulse from without, thus showing its characteristic as the receptive or female side.

Now, in past Universes a process of development has gone on similar to that which is going on in the present world to-day; in those past Universes minds were developed as we develop minds now, and their process of development will be clearer when you follow the process of development amongst ourselves. The minds that developed in those preceding Universes, that passed into Nirvâna, that passed out of Nirvâna again at the beginning of the present age, have many names both in *The Secret Doctrine* and in other books. Let us take the name of "Sons of Mind," because it describes their most salient characteristic. They are sometimes spoken of under the name of Kumâras, which means "youths," sometimes they are called Solar Pitris; but I prefer to take the name most often used in *The Secret Doctrine*, where, of course, you get it in the Sanskrit form, Mânasa Putra; we will take it in English as "Sons of the Mind." They have developed Intelligence. Now, what is Intelligence? Intelligence is the result of vital activity working in a particular form of matter, and developing connecting links between the external Universe and itself. It is a thing of slow growth; it is made by experience; it is evolved, it does not come into existence suddenly. Intelligence is the outcome of these repeated contacts, and of the working of life on the contacts; so that you never can get Intelligence apart from organism. You have something which may be called the Supreme Life, but it is a mistake to speak of It then as Intelligence; It is higher and deeper and sublimer than anything we know as Intelligence, and Its processes are far beyond and above everything that we call thought. Thought always consists in this linking together of the external and the internal, of making ideal links between the two, and hence images—ideas, as we call them; and Intelligence is only developed by the Supreme Life manifesting Itself as what we, for want of a better word, are obliged to call Spirit in the English tongue—Âtmâ is the familiar name in our own philosophy—by thus manifesting Itself in the subtlest form, and then gradually working through matter and thereby evolving what we call Intelligence—that is, all these connecting links that go to build mental faculties.

This process, then, had gone on in a past age so far as these great Sons of Mind are concerned; these mighty Spiritual Intelligences had accomplished what we are aiming at now. They are the successful men of past ages, who have developed into perfect men, perfect Intelligences, and now are, so to speak, co-operating in the building of a new race, co-operating in the production of a new humanity. But up to the point at which we are they had taken no part in this evolution that had been going on—the physical side, the evolution of form. Now, from These is to come a second line, from the Sons of Mind, Lords of Light, They are called sometimes Pillars of Light, and so on; These, coming down to the Earth when the Tabernacles were ready to receive Them, came to give the necessary impulse in order that at this point of junction a new individual might arise, and afforded the active, impelling, positive energy.

You remember at the beginning of the second volume of *The Secret Doctrine*, those Stanzas called the Stanzas of Dzyan, which deal with the Evolution of Man. They have been said lately by Mr. Coleman to be purely modern productions; but they were never found out in modern writings until Madame Blavatsky found them. But leave that to return to this. You will find it said that when these Sons of Mind came down, "from their own Rûpa they filled the Kâma." That is why I was obliged to trouble you with this word, because I wanted to quote that particular Stanza: "From their own Rûpa they filled the Kâma." Coming down to animal-man they threw part of Their own nature into him, filling the Kâma wherein the germ of sensation and feeling had been evolved, and They contributed to that the spark of intelligence. And so again in one of those same Stanzas it is said: "Some projected a spark." The more careful readers amongst you may remember it is said: "Some entered. . . . Those who entered became Arhats." Those are the great Teachers of Humanity in the earlier days of our Race—the fourth and the fifth Races, and the third and a half. The Great Teachers—Those who took this infant Humanity under their care, and trained it, Those who absolutely entered into these bodies that were prepared, with Their highly developed Intelligencies—were the mighty Adepts of the past; They formed what were called the nurseries of Adepts for the present age; the Great Teachers who came in order that this infant Humanity might be guarded and protected and helped in its earlier stages. With Them, so far as ordinary Humanity is concerned, we need not deal; They entered in and took these bodies as Their vehicles. But They also, some of Them, projected the spark which fell into the kâmic receptacle: Their essence filled it. Now the individual begins where that union takes place. Before that there is no Ego in man; before that there is no soul in man in the full sense of the term, although the word Animal Soul is occasionally used for the feelings, emotions, and so on. The lower Soul this is often called, or the Animal Soul; but the true Ego, that which is capable of achieving immortality, is not there. Remember how that phrase is used sometimes; it has not necessarily immortality in itself, although it has in it the power of achieving immortality, by virtue of its connection with these immortal Sons of Mind, Who have already achieved. Man may become immortal "if he will." That was a phrase used, you may remember, in one of the letters from Master K. H. to Mr. Sinnett, published in *The Occult World;* part of the work of the Society was there said to be to teach man that he may become immortal if he will, not that he necessarily is immortal, but that he may achieve immortality. Immortal in the essence of the Soul? Yes; but not in its developed self-conscious intelligence. For intelligence has to be worked out and built up by slow degrees; intelligence has to be evolved by this spark, working through the matter into which it has come, and unless it works successfully, acquires experience slowly, and gradually builds it up into faculty in the course of that pilgrimage of the Soul that lies in front of our thought, immortality will not be achieved. For it is necessary, in order that immortality may be achieved, that this which is to acquire experience and build up accumulated experiences shall regain unity. That which is compounded does not last; that which is compounded will be at some time disintegrated: only the unit persists. The individual begins at this point, and he is a compound. He will weave into his own existence all these endless experiences, and will become, so to speak, more and more compound, a more and more complex combination. But this has in itself the seed of destruction; everything that thus goes on combining has in it the conditions of disintegration, and the compound disintegrates. How then can this compound achieve immortality? By a process of unification that will form the last stages of its pilgrimage; by that Yoga, or union, which will make it again the One. Having achieved individuality by many, many incarnations, through which this individuality will be built up, it then unifies all these experiences, and by a subtle alchemy extracts as it were a unit experience out of the multiplicity, and in a way beyond words—beyond words because it is beyond brain-experience and thought, but which is not beyond the "sensing" of some who have at least begun the process—this individual evolves into a unity higher than its own combined nature; and while it may be said to lose individuality as we know it, it gains something which is far greater. Without losing the essence of individuality, it re-becomes a unit consciousness, and by that becomes incapable of disintegration and achieves its final immortality. But here is the beginning point—and on that I want to lay a good deal of stress—that it begins then, that before that the Ego which is now in each of you was not in existence as Ego, any more than the plant which will develop from a germ, if the germ be fertilised, is in existence before that fertilisation takes place. True, that which will form it exists, because there is no increase either of energy or of matter; but the combination which makes the new individual does not exist until the junction has taken place, and the Ego does not exist before this union has taken place. It is there that originates the individual. You will forgive me for repeating that so often. But this is the point where the mistake comes in, and where there is so much confusion in thought; and it is because of that that I am laying stress upon it, in order that you may have clearly in your minds this fact; that individuals begin in each Manvantara or Age, that the purpose of each Universe is the evolution of individuals, that the Universe comes into existence in order that individuals may be born, that it is maintained in existence in order that individuals may be evolved, that when it passes out of manifestation its harvest is the perfected individuals who regain unity and outlast the Universe, passing into what is called Nirvâna, to re-emerge for a new Universe as Sons of Mind, if in the former Universe they have been completely successful. There are other intermediate stages, points where failure may come in, and where evolution may have to be taken up again as it were midway, points of failure in one Universe that do not throw back the fallen, as Master K. H. pointed out, to the beginning of things again, but are such as to allow them to take up their evolution at the point where it ceased. The failures of one age become, so to speak, the pioneers of another. But leaving those complications out of consideration, the harvest of every Universe is these triumphant individuals, who have evolved unity out of diversity, and thus have achieved their immortality.

Realizing that, then, let us take our individual and see what kind of an entity this is at its origin. And I think I will throw in here a very, very brief digression, which will make it a more living thing to you. Take one of the lower animals. Now we will come to the domesticated. I mentioned that with regard to the wild animal there is the germ of mind, but very little that you can really call mind. Suppose you take an animal and domesticate it, and suppose you domesticate it for generations, you will have handed on in the three bodies of that animal—the physical, the astral, and the kâmic—you will have handed on a very definite heredity; and if these individuals are domesticated time after time you will find greater and greater intelligence, as it may be called, evolving.

Now, supposing that you take a puppy, and supposing that from that puppy's birth you keep it continually with yourselves, and you do not permit it to associate with the lower creatures, but you keep it with yourselves. Some lonely person, for instance, takes a puppy, and it is always with him or her; what is the result? The result is that in that puppy, as it grows up, there is developed a startling amount of some quality that you are forced to call Intelligence. You will develop in it a limited reason; you will develop in it a limited memory; you will develop in it a limited judgment. Now, these are qualities of the mind, not qualities of Kâma. How is it that in this lower animal these qualities are developed? They are developed artificially by the playing upon it of the human intelligence. To that animal the mind in you to some extent plays the part which the Son of Mind plays to Humanity; and thrown out from the comparatively developed Intelligence in man, these rays, these energetic rays of mental influence, vitalize the germ in the Kâma of the animal and so produce artificially, as it were, an nfant mind.

Now I say that, in order that you may realise more clearly perhaps than otherwise you would, the first slow stages of the growth of mind. Let me say that this process is not good for the animal, and it is not good for the human being who does it. Neither the one nor the other is the better for the process, in fact very often both are exceedingly the worse, and it is not a wholesome practice—this over-stimulation of the domesticated animal and this artificial forcing of a mental life for which the animal body is not yet fitted, for which the animal nervous system has not yet developed the proper natural basis, and in which it is really forced, in a kind of artificial hot-house, to the detriment of the creature, and probably to its retardation in a later stage of its existence.

But it is well to remember that there is no such thing as a break in nature; every evolution is sequential, and it is therefore possible to force evolution in this way, although it be unwise.*

Coming back from my little digression, let me take up again my infant Soul, to whom I will give the name of the baby Ego, and he is very much, as regards his mental capacities, what the new-born

* It is with much inner pleasure that I find that a statement current in Theosophical circles, and repeated by me above, is incorrect in fact. It seems, with regard to some animals at least—as the dog and the cat—that the development caused "by the playing upon it of the human intelligence" is well caused, and lifts the animal forward, so that the germinating individuality does not return to animal incarnation, but awaits elsewhere the period at which its further development shall become possible. The "forcing" is therefore helpful and beneficial, not harmful, and we may rid ourselves of the incongruous idea that, in a universe built on and permeated by Love, the out-welling of compassion and love to our younger relatives is injurious to them. There are a good many Theosophists, I think, who will share my pleasure in getting rid of a view against which one's instinct secretly rebelled.

baby is as regards his power of manifesting these faculties. Of course, the new-born baby has mental faculties which very soon force the brain to prepare itself for their manifestation, so that there is not a real analogy between the two. The want of knowledge, so to speak, in the new-born baby is simply due to the clumsiness of the instrument; the brain is new, and it takes some little time for the links to be set up between the instrument and the player. But the player is there, when you are dealing with our race at the present time, and therefore we have not really the condition in which the Ego itself is in the state of babyhood.

Now this entity which has thus been formed at this junction of the two lines, and which I call the baby Ego, is absolutely ignorant. It has no mind, it has no thought, it has nothing more than the sensations it gets from Kâma at present, except the power of evolving which it has received from the stimulating spark of the Son of Mind. Sensations are there; it has to make the link which we call perception. How will that link be made? The sensation will be caused by way of the body through which it has come into contact with some external object. Let us say that the body, by the mouth, comes upon an external object which gives rise to a pleasant sensation of taste—something which is sweet. The animal of course has developed this already, and in the body it will be a habit that when it sees this thing, or feels hunger, it will go towards it. The baby Ego will experience the sensation which is pleasurable, but it will only be a momentary sensation and at first apparently nothing more—a little impact on this germ of mind; over and over again such an impact will take place. At last there is set up in this baby Ego by this repetition a connecting link between the external object that gives rise to a pleasant sensation and the pleasant sensation, and it will thus make its first *thought*. This connecting link between the external and the internal, between the contact which comes from an outside object and the pleasure which that contact gives, will be what is called a "percept," and you have in perception the first activity of the mind; when this perception has been repeated over and over and over and over again, it will be remembered, and conscious memory begins.

Built up in this baby by these repeated contacts, and repeated pleasurable sensations, and repeated connections between the object and the sensation, at last memory will develop, which is the ideal contact; the idea is built out of a number of these sensations. And that faculty of memory will be a faculty of the baby Ego which will be evolved by these constant experiences; and it will take a long time evolving—perhaps a whole life, or part of a life. I cannot measure it off; but I want you to realise that it is a thing which will take a considerable time, that the memory will be a thing which will need much experience at this early stage, before it will really become recognisable and workable.

There are human beings even at the present time in which this faculty of the Soul is so little developed that it will not last over even twelve hours, and in which their view of the world is quite different in the morning and in the evening. Some of the lowest aborigines in Australia in whom the spark has burned very low, in whom it has not developed and grown, are on record as having so little memory that they cannot remember through the course of a whole day, and blankets given away in the evening will be clung to because the night has begun and the night is cold. But when the next morning comes round and the immediate use for the blanket is over, and while they do not want the blanket they do want food—the food is an immediate want, but the blanket won't be wanted till evening—some of them have not sufficiently developed what we should call the idea of invariable sequence in their minds to remember that night will come back again after the day is over, and that the blanket which they do not want while the sun is out they will want when the sun has set. The sunset of yesterday is, so to speak, a past incarnation to them, and they do not carry on the memory through the night; therefore, they will part with their blanket for a mere trifle in the morning, although they will not part with it in the evening—a most striking illustration of the baby sense, if I may so call it, of the Ego which is incarnated in these aborigines. They are dying off very fast, and no English government will be able to keep them alive, because their work is done. A race dies when it is of no more use to the Soul; it becomes sterile when its purpose in the evolution of the Soul is over. For as the Universe only exists for the sake of the Soul, so all these stages in the Universe exist for the Soul, and when there are no more Souls so little developed that such a race is of any use to them, it becomes sterile and gradually disappears. I do not mean when it is helped to disappear by the superior races, though that is often the case; but even if they do not help it to disappear rapidly, it will inevitably disappear slowly on its own account, by the barrenness which falls upon it. It is of no more use, therefore it does not continue.

That illustration may give you some idea of what the spark is like in its early stages, as you find it in these sparks that have burned low and not developed. Memory will be very, very slowly developed, but when it is developed, even in a limited way, you will at once see that an element is present conducing to more rapid growth, because the moment that this baby remembers past experiences it is then beginning to accumulate a little store which will impel it to action without impulse from without. It will have an impulse beginning from within which will lead it to seek experiences. Farther, not until it has memory can it distinguish, in their absence, between pleasurable and painful experiences, good and evil, as it will call them, and so begin to develop in itself a power of comparison and selection, *i.e.*, of judgment, which will serve as a guide for action. Let me take the case of taste, which I chose before. It was pleasurable. Of course, some tastes will be unpleasant, and those will be marked off as painful, to be avoided. So that the Ego will get, as it begins to remember, two classes of things in the outer world; one labelled in its own mind—if I may call it mind at this stage: "pleasure; to be sought, to be followed"; and the other labelled: "painful; to be avoided, to be run away from, to be escaped." And at this stage the Universe, so to speak, will divide itself into two for this baby Ego, things to be run after and things to be run away from. It will not have gone any further than that. Going out into an unknown world where it comes into contact with objects, the first great division will be things that it wants, and things that it does not want; and the wanting or the not wanting will depend on whether it meets something which it desires to repeat because it gives it pleasure, or something which it desires to avoid repeating because it gives it pain. This is the beginning of experience.

In this way it will begin, as it accumulates these experiences of pleasure and of pain, to learn something more; it will begin to learn that this world that it has come into is a very definite kind of thing, and that it has got to accommodate itself to it; it will find some things in it that do not give way, and that if it runs up against those things certain unpleasant results always follow. Memory of course is wanted for this, to notice that always the same thing comes from the same object under the same circumstances; and when sufficient of these sensations have been accumulated to give rise to the definite idea that doing a particular thing will cause pain, *there* is the first glimpse of law, of something external to itself which it cannot overcome, which throws it back, as it were, and gives what it feels as pain, something repellent when it comes against it. So the idea begins to arise that not only are some things to be followed and others to be avoided, but that these things which are to be followed, and which are pleasure-giving, are things which are "good"—which only means at first harmonious—that others are inharmonious and unpleasant, and therefore "evil"; that there is a law of pleasure and of pain to which it must adapt itself if it wants to live in comfort, that nothing that it can do will break this law, and that, therefore, it will be wise to accommodate itself to the law. This observation of sequence will be made by our baby Ego and will give rise to the idea of Law, and of the need to adapt itself to these laws if it is to live at all comfortably. And then a little more will come as the experience goes on; that sometimes a thing begins by giving pleasure and goes on by giving pain—a most confusing experience. Let us cling to our taste. The body of our baby Ego eats and pleasure is felt; because of this it makes the body go on eating till it eats too much. It then finds that by repeating this gratification pain has come where there was pleasure. It makes its body ill; and it gets a new view of the outside Universe—that the gratification of this which began by being pleasurable works out into pain, and that the pleasure which began in flavour may end in most uncomfortable aches; and not only so, but, persisted in, may cause perennial aches which later on it will know as disease. This very much emphasises its idea of law, and it begins to accumulate now a sequential experience of different pleasures and pains, and to realise that it bears a certain relationship to these outside contacts; it learns that it is not the outside object in itself which is pleasure-giving or pain-giving, but some relation that arises between itself and the outside object—a great advance—and that these outside objects are neither pleasure-giving nor pain-giving in themselves, but only in relation to itself, the same thing sometimes giving the one and sometimes giving the other. So that the idea of pleasure and pain, in this further experience of our baby Ego, will go on into the relationships that itself sets up with the outer world, and that change the character of the outside impact from pleasurable to painful. And then the law will begin to take on, as it were, a compelling power, and it will realise that it can adapt itself to this strange external apparent change, and that by adapting itself it can persist in pleasure or persist in pain, and that the pleasure and pain will depend on its attitude to the outer world. And so this next lesson of experience will be learned. And there I must leave my baby Ego for to-night, having reached as far as the recognition of an outer world, the receiving of pleasure and of pain, the recognition of relations, therefrom evolution of memory, evolution of judgment—which recognizes the relationship as having in itself this difference of pleasure and pain—so that we have the beginnings of perception, memory, judgment—three things that are wanting for what we call reason of an elementary kind. Reason only exists in the baby Ego as a mere germ; and we will leave him as he passes through death, carrying with him these germinal mental faculties which he has evolved. We cannot say how much progress would be made in one of these early lives; probably many lives would be needed to arrive at the stage just described. In order to make our study complete in outline, let us take him at the end of his first life, to see the principle underlying *post-mortem* evolution. Let us see him having begun his pilgrimage and passing for the first time through the gate of death. On the other side of that we will leave him to take him up again next week.

PART II.

YOU will remember that last week we left what I called the baby Ego having passed through the gateway of death. Now I spoke of his passing for the first time through the gateway of death, because I wanted to take up for a few moments the *post-mortem* states in order that we might have as it were before us for the rest of the study of the pilgrimage this complete cycle: the life upon earth, the life in the transition state beyond death, the life in the Devachanic state—the life of the Soul properly so-called, the intellectual and intelligent life. Those three stages, being the three divisions of the pilgrimage completing a single period, are repeated over and over and over again, succeeding each other in this definite way, all bearing to each other a definite relation, so that unless we understand each of the three we shall not be able to follow with any intelligence the pilgrimage of the Soul or the growth of the Ego.

When, however, this germinal Ego that I spoke of last week passes for the first time through the gateway of death, it has exceedingly little material for these stages that lie on the other side of that gateway. The first stage is that which may be called—translating the term—the Land of Desire. You will remember that desire is Kâma, and Loka is place; so that this land or place of desire is called, in Theosophical books, Kâma Loka; that is, a place inhabited by Souls still clad in the desire or sensation body that we studied last week. The Ego in this body dwells there for a time—but not only the Ego of man. It is the place where these bodies of sensation and desire survive the physical and the astral bodies; so that you have there these desire or sensation bodies of the lower animals as well as those which are inhabited by the Human Soul.

Now, when our baby Ego is at this very early stage of his life there will be in him a great deal of the lower element of Kâma or desire, and scarcely anything at all of the higher element of Mind. His stay then in this Kâma Loka will be for a considerable period, and all that he will do there is to experience pleasant or painful results according as the life which has been led on the physical plane—which has been led upon earth—has been in accordance with law or discordant with law. The life there is exceedingly limited, and is simply a result from the life upon earth. Nothing new is introduced into it; it is a life in which there is a great deal of repetition, in which an experience is repeated over and over and over again. And this automatic action, as we may call it, is one of the great characteristics of this Kâmic body, or body of sensation. You know how easily habits are set up—habits of the physical body, especially habits which are connected with the passions and with the emotions. The great root of these habits lies in the body of sensation with its peculiarly strong automatic tendencies. Those are impressed on the outer body, although, of course, the habit of repetition in the physical body will also come in to some extent.

When the Soul has passed out of this transitional state it leaves behind it this body of desire, just as in leaving the earth it left the physical body. The bodies belong to certain definite stages in the Universe, and the Soul cannot carry on any body with which it has been clothed further than the stage in the Universe to which that body belongs. It cannot carry the physical body away from the physical plane; it cannot carry the astral body out of the lower astral world; it cannot carry this body of sensation out of the transitional state, known as the land of sensation or desire. And when it has worn it out sufficiently to allow it to escape—when it has exhausted, so to speak, this body of desire, which has been nourished in the sensational life of earth—then it passes on into a higher condition, into a higher sphere, where the whole of its work is the work of the mind, all higher aspirations, all thoughts which are devoid of passion and of appetite, everything which is intellectual as distinguished from what is passional, all the higher emotions which have in them this element of mind as well as the lower element of passion—these, purified from passion, will be carried on into this higher world. And the length of the stay of the Soul in that world depends on the amount which during its earth-life it has accumulated of mental experiences, and of experiences of the higher emotions, of the artistic faculties, and so on—everything, in fact, which has to do with the mind. Understanding that, you will see at once that when the Soul first passes through the gateway of death there will be scarcely anything for it to carry on into this higher condition, hardly any experiences which it can use for the development, as it were, of mental faculty. Still, the very few experiences that it has acquired during its first life in the body, which are not kâmic, will be carried on. What will be its work, then, in this higher world? It will be to extract from these separated mental experiences their essence, and to transmute that essence by working upon it with this energy of the Soul, transmute that essence into mental faculty, or mental ability. The work that the Soul accomplishes when it is out of the body, when it can no longer gather fresh experiences, when it has lost the three bodies through which experiences can alone be collected, the work of the Soul is then to take up the mental images remaining from these experiences, and, working on them, to take out of them their essence. Just in the same way that a chemist might take a number of chemical elements, might throw them into a crucible, and then, purifying them from dross, might extract the elements themselves and combine them in the crucible; so does this chemist, as it were—the Soul—by the alchemy of its own mental ability, the thought power which it has developed, working on these accumulated and separated experiences, throwing them into the crucible of the mind, extract from them their essence, and then taking that essence it assimilates it, makes it part of itself, works it into its own nature, or—to use the phrase that I used two or three times last week—weaves these separated experiences into itself, and so begins to make a real garment of the Soul, which is the character of the Soul, and which will reappear as character when it comes back to earth. Everything that the Soul brings with it of mental faculty, everything that is born, as we say, with the child, the powers of the mind which the child shows—the whole of these are brought back by the Soul as the result of its workings on past experiences while it is living in the world of the Soul, the world that we call Devachan in our Theosophical literature, which simply means the land of bliss. As I say, then, in these early experiences there will be very little for the Soul to work upon in this blissful land; but when it comes back, even after this first period is completed, and comes to be born for the second time upon earth, it will have what it did not have at the beginning—a little germ of mental faculty. That is the small result in faculty which it has brought back by working on the few experiences that it accumulated during its previous life. It will start, then, at a certain advantage in this second period of its pilgrimage; it will start with certain tools, as it were, ready made to its hand, which it has fashioned for itself during this interlude in the world of the Soul; it will come back with a nascent memory, with a nascent power of comparison, very, very small certainly, but still, so to speak, better than none; and it will work through that on the new experiences that come to it by way of sensation from the outer world.

Through this life, then, again it will pass, having this advantage now, that it has a little mental faculty to go upon which it can increase. As it goes on experiences increase, its power to receive the experiences being greater, and this mental element mixing itself up with the emotional and the passional nature. So that we now speak of the mind, or, as we call it, Manas—the word from which our own word man is derived, and which really means the thinker, the great characteristic of the man being that he thinks. This Manas, then, now coming back, small as its powers are, will modify and change the whole of the kâmic nature, the passional nature; and all that this Ego now experiences will have in it the two elements—the element of passion which belongs to its passional nature, and the element which comes from this mind which is developing, which tends gradually more and more to observe, and to compare, and to make record of its experiences, and to store them up in order that it may direct its action by them. At first all the actions will grow from outer attraction; presently against the outer attraction there will be working the images of past experiences. So that, to take up the illustration that I used last week of taste, when there is a strong attraction from without of a taste which it knows will be pleasurable, excess will be guarded against by the mental image which has been preserved of the pains that in previous experiences were the result of over-gratification of taste. So that now you will have this double element. And remember that the element of the mind is increasing, while the other element is more or less stationary. As the Soul passes from life to life, and in each life accumulates experiences, in each transitional stage after death suffers from the animal appetites which hold it prisoner from going on into the happier world, and then in that happier world works upon the experiences and changes them into faculties, it will always have an accumulating stock of faculty, an accumulating store of memories, while the outer attractions will remain comparatively the same, and action will be more and more directed by reason and less and less directed by appetite.

Now, understanding that you will be fairly able, I think, to trace, so to speak, the stages of this pilgrimage of the Soul: you see the elements that enter into the pilgrimage; you see the tools with which the Soul will have to work improvements if it uses its experiences well in the successive incarnations; and you will also understand that on the accumulation of these experiences, and the working upon those experiences in the blissful land, will depend the more rapid or the slower growth of the faculties of the Soul—that is, whether it will grow rapidly, or will grow slowly or moderately, whether the pilgrimage shall be comparatively swift or very much delayed. You will see also how the Soul may often be thrown back, how a very strong attraction from without may overbear, say, a comparatively small store of accumulated experiences; and then the Soul will make a mistake, will go against the law, and will suffer.

How should we regard such an experience when we are studying this pilgrimage of the Soul? Is it a matter for very great regret? Is it a matter for extreme grief and sorrow?

Think it out for yourselves, and you will see the way in which this wider view of life will regard any mistake, any blunder, any fall, any sin. Sin is disharmony with law. So long as the law is not understood desire will constantly be drawing the Soul outward without regard to this law of which it knows nothing, and striking on the law it will feel pain. Suppose, then, that it has not accumulated a sufficient store of these painful experiences to make it realize the presence of the law; or suppose that, having accumulated sufficient experience to recognise the presence of the law, it has not accumulated sufficient to overbear the strong drawing of attraction to the external object; then the very experience of wrong-doing is a necessary stage in its education.

For the pain that results from the wrong-doing will add to the store of experience that the Soul is gradually accumulating, and will make it stronger against the temptation in the future by this new suffering which it has found must inevitably result from coming into conflict with the law. So that instead of being heart-broken over a failure, those who see from life to life and look on the pilgrimage of the Soul as a great whole, and not simply in the fragments that ordinary persons see in looking at it, they can see with calmness these blunders that the Soul makes, knowing that they are the result of insufficient experience, and that the very fall will supply an added experience which will help the Soul to stand when it comes into a similar position in the future. And there is no more reason for extreme sorrow over these blunders of the growing Soul than, to use a simile that I have often used before, there is reason for the mother to break her heart because the child may stumble when it is learning to walk. If the child is hurt she may feel sorrow for the child's pain, but she certainly will not go into a state of frantic despair about it. She will know that these tumbles are a necessary part of the education of the child in gaining equilibrium, and will know that every tumble it has will make the tumbles of the future less likely to occur.

Now, that is not a callous way of looking at things; it is a wise way; and as knowledge grows wisdom gives balance to contemplate calmly many things that otherwise would be distressing and disturbing in the very highest degree. Calmness, which is a characteristic of wisdom, comes from this wider vision which is able to understand causes as well as see effects, and which understands how that which to-day seems sad will work out for good in days to come.

One other distinction that we want to realise as to the principles at work in this pilgrimage of the Soul is that the kâmic element with which the Ego is encircled, constantly giving rise to desire, is that which is always making links which bring it back to birth. Every desire that you have for something down here survives death, remains behind you in the transition state until you return for re-incarnation, and draws you back to re-birth as soon as you have exhausted in the blissful land the accumulated experiences of the mind whieh you work upon in that region of the Universe. So to speak, when the body drops from it the Ego, having accumulated sufficient materials for its work, has the tendency to leave the Earth and assimilate what it has gained through these agencies which exist in the desire body. It leaves earth behind, being drawn by the stronger mental forces onward, where it has to work in the region of ideas. When its store is exhausted, then the desire links re-assert their power, and the Ego having finished, having got through all the mental experiences in the blissful land, feels again these links of desire reasserting their power, and it is drawn back by them to re-incarnation, and attached by those links of desire to all the objects of desire with which they are connected.

Now, the especial reason why I mention this is that I hear so many people when they are dealing with re-incarnation say, "I don't want to come back." It is of no use having a theory that you do not want to come back, if you are making these desire links to things on the physical and on the kâmic planes. So long as you want anything which the world can give you your Ego *does* want to come back, and must come back whether you think you want it or not. The fact that it desires something here shows this fundamental craving for return, and the mere feeling of weariness, which is the outcome of a tired brain and of a consciousness working in that tired brain, has absolutely nothing to do with the inevitable destiny of the Ego. The brain which is tired certainly will not come back; it will go to pieces on the earth to which it belongs, and the tiredness which makes people say, "I don't want to come back," is the tiredness of this outside body, the desire to escape from the painful things that have made an impression upon it, and so on. The real desire is shown by the attachment to the things of earth, by the wish for one thing or another, the wish for ease, the wish for pleasure, the wish for social consideration, the wish for the praise of men, the wish for everything with which men's and women's lives are filled well-nigh to the brim at the present time. For persons who are full of desire in this way to say, "I don't want to come back," is simply to show a lack of understanding. They must come back until there is nothing here which has the slightest attraction for them. When nothing here attracts them, when praise and blame are exactly the same to them, when they do not mind whether in the outside world they are rich or poor, when they do not mind whether they are what people call happy or unhappy, when the whole outside life is an absolute matter of indifference, when nothing can shake their peace or bring the slightest ruffle of any kind over the emotional nature, then that Soul is ready to go on; but so long as any of these things have the slightest influence, so long these links are being made and must draw the Soul back to fresh experiences of earth.

Manas itself does not make these links; it makes

them through Kâma, and it makes them where the desire even for intellectual things comes in, but not by pure abstract thinking, which is its own special work—that is to say, it is Manas pure and simple which makes links bringing us back to re-birth, it is Kâma-Manas, which is the form of Manas working amongst the great masses of people to-day. Manas itself, which comes out now and again in absolutely abstract thinking, does not make links which draw to re-birth. But inasmuch as almost all intellectual effort here is very largely carried on with the kâmic element, and has worked through the brain, which is the vehicle of Kâma-Manas, most intellectual effort will have in it the desire element, and so will bring the Soul back for fresh experiences upon the earth.

As to the way in which it works: it works by what we may call the creative power of thought. The whole world is the outcome of the Divine Thought. Everything which we know as phenomenal is the mere outside appearance which has in it the inner and living reality of thought. All outside appearance is but the form which the thought takes for expression on these lower planes; and the whole Universe is nothing more than a Divine Thought in manifestation. That Divine, that God-like element is in man, and it works through Manas and is the creative element. The more of that there is in the activity of a person the more is he a creative energy in the world.

Every thought makes to itself a form. Every time that you think a form is made in your mental atmosphere. A passing thought will only have a very transitory form; a thought which is constantly repeated will have a form which by these repetitions becomes stronger and stronger and more and more permanent, so that according to the fixity and the motives of your thoughts will be the life of the thought-forms that you are continually generating around you.

If you refer to a letter in *The Occult World*, written by Master K. H. to Mr. Sinnett, you will see that he points out that when a thought goes out and takes form it is vivified or entered into by an Elemental, and the character of the Elemental will be according to the character of the thought, and accordiug to the motive that has inspird the thought. If the thought be a good one—for instance, directed to human service with a desire to serve—then it will be helped from outside by this Elemental, which is of a good and a pure type, and the thought will be a force for good, reacting on the person who has thought it, and reacting on all those who come within the sphere of his influence. So that every thought which is loving and helpful lives in the world of thought as a useful influence. And supposing that these good thoughts are directed towards people, then they go to the people to whom the will directs them and, so to speak, encircle them with a protective and aiding power. And it is a real thing that every good and kind thought that you have of a person, every wish for their benefit, every desire for their happiness, is an actual living thing that goes to that person as a living entity, and lives, as it were, in connection with the person towards whom you have directed it as a protective agency, warding off danger and drawing good towards that person to whom you have sent this angel of your thought.

So, again, with all evil thoughts, thoughts which have in them the element of hate, of revenge, of passion—those draw to themselves from the outer world Elementals which increase this energy. So that an evil thought directed against a person is an absolutely mischievous agent, which may injure him either in physical health, in the astral body, or in any part of his body or mind. Suppose the person has nothing in him which in any sense forms a link with this thought of yours, then the thought will be thrown back, and will return to yourself and strike you to your own injury. Suppose, however, that the person has, what most people have, some little fault in himself which may make a link with this thought of yours, then the evil thought attaches itself to the person and injures that person in some part of his nature. Therefore is it that everything which is of the nature of evil thought consciously directed towards a person has been called, and rightly called, Black Magic. A thought of revenge or of anger which is directed towards any person with a view to injure him is essentially of the nature of Black Magic. And the greater the power of the person who does it, and the greater the knowledge of the person who does it, the greater is their crime for which they have to answer to the Law. In this way, then, the Soul works by these thought-forms. First these thought-forms, then their Elementals, working back upon the Soul that generates them, as well as working in the outer world; these go on with the Soul into Devachan, so far as they are pure in their nature, and make the faculty of which I spoke, being, as it were, moulded into faculty; and then, coming back, the physical body is moulded by way of the astral to manifest this character, which has taken to itself, by means of these thought-forms, certain definite shapes. So that it is perfectly true that the outer body of a person will show something of his character. That body is physically built on the aggregated thought-forms which have been transformed by the alchemy that I spoke of into definite faculties, and these, having their characteristic forms, will mould the shaping of the outer body. And it is perfectly true that when you are dealing with the general shape of the brain you will have that brain developed in certain regions, according to the character of the Ego that inhabits it. The mistake is to suppose that it is the tabernacle which makes the tenant; it is the tenant who builds the tabernacle. So that while you have the two correlated the one to the other we must not begin at the wrong end, and believe that the master-builder is made by his house; he builds himself the dwelling in which, in his coming incarnation, he will have to live.

One other point as regards our back-coming Ego. You will notice I am not tracing him life by life. I am giving you general principles which will work through large numbers of lives. These stages being passed through, what circumstances will our Ego come back into? That will depend upon the circumstances that during his past life he caused upon earth; according to the happiness or misery he caused upon earth in a past incarnation, so will be the circumstances in which he will find himself when he comes back to earth.

Suppose, for instance, that a man whose influence

extends over large numbers of people spreads happiness around him on every side. That is a distinct effect that he has worked, and it will govern the condition in which he will be born in his next life. This happiness that he spreads amongst large numbers of his fellows is a seed which will spring up as happy circumstances for his next incarnation. Sowing happiness he will reap happiness; sowing pain he will reap pain. If he causes a great deal of physical suffering in his life, he will reap much physical misery in some following incarnation. If he spreads around him much mental distress and trouble, he will reap mental distress and trouble in the circumstances that come in his way. Mind, these are things he cannot alter. They are fixed future events, so to speak, when he leaves the earth. These are the things that can be predicted of him with fair certainty, because these are seeds that are left which have to grow up each after its own kind. Over these he has no power; they are there, and he has got to live amongst them.

Now, you may have a man who is not a good man morally, but who has yet spread a very large amount of happiness amongst people, say, of a physical kind; he will reap physical happiness in his next incarnation. You may find a good man who by lack of knowledge has spread a great deal of misery, and he will reap physical suffering in his next incarnation. You have to distinguish, if you want to understand, between these different agencies of the Soul. According to his desires and his will, so will be his faculties—his own personal possessions, or individual possessions rather, if I may call them so; according to what he has sown upon earth will be his harvest upon earth when he returns. So that all these circumstances of happiness or of misery will be the result of the happiness or the misery that he has spread in previous incarnations: they will come back to him as environment, as circumstances.

Now I come to my next point. You must remember the pilgrimage of the Soul is very long, and a lecture is very short, so that I am obliged to run somewhat rapidly from one subject to another. The next point at which I must make a moment's pause is on our Ego when he has become more experienced. He is no longer a baby, nor even a child, nor even a youth; he is a mature Ego and he is becoming wise. With this wisdom of his he is bringing back more and more faculty, he is bringing back more and more memory, he will make for himself instruments which will be able to express greater and greater capacity, and a time will come in this pilgrimage of his in which his constant efforts to impress on these lower tabernacles his own ever-lengthening memory of past experiences will become more and more successful. His will having grown very strong, will tell considerably upon his lower nature. What we call the voice of conscience will begin to make itself heard with more imperative force. Now, conscience is this memory of the Soul expressing itself in the lower nature; it comes with authority, and the lower nature feels the authoritative sound in it: "You ought to do this; you ought not to do that." And sometimes the lower nature will challenge it, not being able to undestand where this authority comes from. The authority lies in the Soul, which is trying to make the lower nature go its way; it is using its own past experience to prevent the lower nature being led astray by the outside objects, by its mistaken deductions, by its very incomplete experiences. And it is speaking constantly to this lower nature, and constantly the lower nature does not hear. In all the clatter and jangle of the body in which it is living it finds it is very difficult to make its voice heard coming from the higher planes. But the voice of the conscience is always this voice of the Soul, speaking out of its memory. And if you think that out at your leisure you will see how it is that conscience will sometimes speak wrongly as to choice of action, but always with the sense of, "You ought to do." The reason that it sometimes speaks wrongly as to action is because the experience is still a limited experience. The reason why it is always imperative is because that limited experience is the only guide which Manas has, and it is the best guide even though it be imperfect. A man therefore does wisely always to obey his conscience. It is the best decision which experience enables the Soul to make, and if it be faulty, it is faulty because of the want of experience. If you obey it, when it blunders you will gain the lacking experience; and you will suffer more if you do not obey it. By following some other rule which is not the rule of your own inner Self, speaking from its own experience, you will be obeying an external law, which, speaking from without, is not to be relied upon to develop your Soul. The Soul is developed by experience, not by compulsion; and an outer law, however good it may be, does not, being a compulsory power, add to the inner forces of the Soul; therefore is it of comparatively small value in evolution, far less than the voice of conscience, even when the conscience is faulty.

Now taking that, let us come back from that slight digression to our Ego. It has become comparatively mature, it is getting wiser. Getting wiser it wants to escape from this constant succession of births and of deaths of which it is beginning to get a little tired. It has gone through it so often that it has accumulated a great deal of experience, and many things in the world no longer attract it. Everything they can give it, it has gathered; why should it want to repeat its experience of them? The taste has disappeared because the experience has been obtained; and as this Soul comes back there will be a number of things in the outer world that will no longer attract, and that it will turn aside from with a sense of weariness and disgust. These things will first be the things of the senses, which are the soonest worn out, and it will go more and more towards the things of the mind, more and more towards the things of the intellect, accumulating a larger and larger store for its Devachanic life, a greater and greater accumulation on which it is going to work. So that the life in Devachan will be longer and longer, the Soul working out these greater stores which it carries with it from this earthly life. Coming back then again, having had these long Devachanic interludes, it comes back with this ever-increasing distaste for the lower desires, and the links with objects of the sense become feebler and feebler. Its knowledge enables it to recognise the transitory and illusory character of earthly things, and it breaks the links of desire by knowledge; knowing that they pass, it refuses to be attached to them, and so exhausts these links which inevitably draw it back to earth so long as they last. Instead of setting up great numbers of these, it creates only thought-forms of the pure intellect, and the pure reason, and the pure thought, which do not tie it to these transitory things of the earth. And it may break these links in two ways—by knowledge in the way that I described; or also it may break them by catching glimpses of higher and greater realities—the spiritual realities as we say—and that mightier attraction, overbearing the attraction to earth, will draw the desires upwards, purifying them as they ascend. So that at last all the lower element of desire which is for the lower self will be got rid of, and there will be present only the desire to work because the work is useful, to work because the work is duty, to work because others need the service, and so on.

You may thus get rid of the personal element in desire, which is the binding element for return, and in one of two ways: either by a distinctly intellectual recognition of the transitory character of the objects and the exhausting of desire by knowledge, or by the burning up of desire by devotion, and the deliberate sacrifice of everything to the higher ideal of life which is to become its compelling power.

The time will come in the growth of this Ego when it will realize then that the lower earth has nothing which is worth having. By knowledge, by devotion, or by both it has broken these links. What then will be the nature of the life to be lived, when it is establishing no new links to bring it back to birth? It may be a very active life, employed constantly in working amongst men; for it is not action that binds men to birth, but the desire which causes action. In desire, and not in act, lies this link which draws the Ego back to birth. Suppose then that during a life of very great activity there is no desire; suppose every action that is performed is performed because it is right to be done; suppose that when it is performed, the Ego concerns itself no more about it; suppose it has no wish for the result of that action, either good, or bad, or indifferent; suppose that when the action is performed there is no link which binds the Soul to it in any way, that it remains absolutely indifferent to the fruit of action, as it is technically called, and works, not because it wants to gain anything, but because it wants to serve and because it recognises that it is one with the All, and therefore must discharge perfectly everything which the law demands of it in the particular place in the world in which it may be. Freedom of the Soul, then, depends on whether you want to bring about a result by your action, because the result is desirable, or merely because you want to be in harmony with law, because you recognise yourself as part of the All, because you recognise yourself as a channel of the law. If you are nothing more than that, if everything that you do is done because it is duty, if you act neither for pleasure nor pain, neither from love nor hatred, neither from attraction nor repulsion, neither for gain nor loss, then, there being no desire, no link is made; in the doing of the action you are part of the One and the All; and That cannot be bound by these links to rebirth, so that the question of outer activity does not affect in itself the freedom of the Soul. I grant, of course, to the full that people need the stimulus of desire in order to make them act, until they have reached this higher stage where action is perfectly performed for duty's sake. It cannot be reached at a bound, it cannot be reached by its intellectual recognition, it cannot be reached even by saying that it is desirable; it can only be reached by the inner growth of the Ego, which makes it really fundamentally indifferent to all the things which attract the masses of mankind. So long as there is attraction, that is needed for the performance of duty. It is only when the lower nature is entirely the instrument of the higher that a man will lead a life of great activity without the smallest wish to see anything which may flow from his acts; and when that point is reached, he has achieved his freedom, when that is done, Karma for him—save the great Karma of the Universe—is at an end. Individual Karma for him is burnt up, burnt up in these fires of knowledge and of devotion which prevent him establishing any links with the earth, and he therefore makes no fetters which bind him to the wheel of birth and of death. The burning up of Karma in this fire of devotion means that you throw into the fire every action of your life, and like a sacrifice it is burnt up and changed.

Let me give you one illustration only to show you how this change may occur in the higher spiritual life.

There may be a thing which will bring suffering. The Soul which is nearing its liberation is willing to accept that suffering which still it feels; it throws the suffering on to the altar of devotion; the fire of devotion burns up the suffering, and the Soul feels joy in its gift. But that suffering is not lost; it is changed in the fire, and it becomes spiritual energy, which the Great Lodge can use for the helping of man—the voluntary acceptance of pain as a sacrifice to the Masters is changed by that fire of devotion into spiritual energy for the helping of the world. There is the underlying truth of the doctrine of what is called vicarious atonement; not the legal thing that the Churches have sometimes taught, but the sacrifice of a great Soul, which bears suffering and offers it for the spiritual life of the world, so that it shall be changed in the fire of love and come back as spiritual energy to be spread over the whole of the world for the raising and the helping of man.

The Soul, then, thus achieving liberation, comes to the period of choice of which you hear so much. Being free it has a right to choose, and it may either pass onwards into higher types of life, or it may elect to remain within the sphere of earth in order that it may directly help in the freeing of other Souls. That is, of course, the Great Renunciation of which every now and then you catch glimpses in the Theosophical writings; that is the choice of the liberated Soul; it is free, but it remains within the sphere of earth in order to help. It may choose that, by renunciation of its right to go on. It is not bound to earth, but by a voluntary renunciation it remains there with some of the disadvantages, so to speak, which belong to the material existence, for the sake of helping others and carrying on this evolution of the Race.

Where a Soul has thus accomplished its pilgrimage, where stage after stage it has developed mind, where stage after stage it has purified intellect, when it has got rid of desire, when it has become a liberated

Soul, when it has renounced the going onward for the sake of humanity, when it has remained within this sphere of earth for helping man until the cycle of humanity is completed, then, entering into Nirvâna, there comes the state of All-consciousness, of bliss which no words are able to describe. And then when the time comes for a new manifestation, when the beginning of a new Manvantara approaches, then this Soul which had achieved its liberation comes forth as a Son of Mind, in order in due time to generate mind in a new humanity, to be the Teacher of that humanity in its infancy, its guide in its maturity, rising Manvantara after Manvantara higher and higher. For the pilgrim Soul which began in the germ-union that I described, which went on by accumulating experiences, which then from these experiences extracted their essence, which then got rid of the desires which made it separate, and which unified itself once more, becoming a unit consciousness in a mysterious way which can not even be sensed until at least the lower grades of the higher consciousness have been experienced during earth-life by rising out of the body and learning what it is to be an Intelligence working without the shackles of the brain—such a Soul thus having worked through its pilgrimage and regained unity, shakes off the compound individuality, retaining the essence of it which it extracts; being a unit it is incapable of disintegration, it is for ever immortal—the Soul has achieved its immortality, and through all Universes to come it is one of the Workers, one of the Builders, one with God in work for the worlds.

Printed by Percy Lund, Humphries & Co., The Country Press, Bradford; and 3, Amen Corner, London, E.C.